WARNING

Due to content this book is intended for mature audiences only (18+) and contains explicit descriptions of violence and intense sexual situations and rape.

W9-AOW-300

TABLE OF CONTENTS

The Journals Trilogy
#ONE

ANGUISH

BY
D.M. EARL

Evelyn,
Take the journey
with Quinn thru
her past.

DM Earl

COPYRIGHT

ACKNOWLEDGEMENTS

There are two women I would like to thank. Since I have started working with them, they have been my constant in this Indie World. Putting up with my OCD craziness, and through every process involved in getting my book out there.

Margreet Asselbergs, my Illustrator of everything design related. She has produced five of my six covers (Two haven't even been released as of yet). Along with that, she has designed my brand, Facebook banners, helped me with my swag and designed a kick-ass banner for signings. But more than that, she has been such an awesome support and someone I am proud to call my friend. We finally met at the Detroit Indie Mashup this year and I will tell you it was an honor to share a table with her. She is a wonderful woman and an example of how to present yourself in this Indie World. She puts up with me and never tells me no, even when she's busy as hell. Margreet always makes time for me and her work is out of this world.

Dana Hook is my Editor. That in itself is a full time job because I am new at this. Her job is not easy at all because I have no formal writing background. I write down what I want the story to be, go through it and pass it over to Dana to work her magic. That she does, but let me tell you, we bump heads all the time. She is as outspoken and determined as I am, if not more. That is why I appreciate her so much. She is never afraid to tell me like it is and tell me when shit doesn't work. This woman has more heart and soul than anyone else I have met in this Indie Author world. She will fight for you 'til the end if she believes in you. For those she calls her "girls" we will never have to worry because Dana always has our backs and to me, that is enough. Thanks Boss for all you do for me, even when you might not think I appreciate it. It initially hurts sometimes when you rip apart my words, but I will tell you that most of the time, you are right. Yeah, I said it. I got lucky finding you, Dana, and know I'm blessed.

Laura B and Sarah, my PA's. Thanks for all that you are doing to allow me to write more as you manage everything else. It means the world to me.

Karen (Blondie), your friendship has become priceless to me. Thanks for going through this first book and being honest. More importantly, thanks for your friendship and for always being there with a kind word or just checking in to see how I'm doing. You are an amazing person.

To all my Author friends, which is a list that continues to grow, I appreciate each and every one of you. Your kind words, advice, or just following your posts, have helped me to grow.

Bloggers, you all ROCK! Because of you all, with your dedication and hard work, my name is getting out there and it is all because of you guys. Thank you for your love of reading and helping Indie Authors out. Never think for a moment I take you for granted because I don't.

Finally, my "sista," Patti, who from the beginning of this journey has been stellar in her support of this dream. Never has she let me doubt myself and has pushed me forward into the unknown, telling me that I am on the right road. Patti, thanks for always having my back and supporting me. I luv ya like a sista.

DEDICATIONS

To my husband Chuck, who is my strongest supporter, who has put up with all the crazy stuff since I started down this road, wanting to live my dream of writing. He allows me to strive for the stars each and every day.

To every Reader who has reached out to me to let me know they enjoyed my work, left a comment on my Facebook page, or sent me a personal message, Thank You. You all have given me something I can never repay you for— Support, and as long as I have that, I will continue on with this journey of writing stories and hoping with all my heart that you all enjoy them.

Enjoy this Ride we call Life!

PROLOGUE

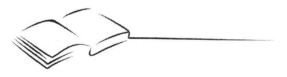

How the fuck did I end up like this; afraid of my own shadow, living isolated from the entire world? Yes, I'm a crazy fuck, but I can at least get out of this depressing house and run a business. I manage to socialize with people, but they don't know me—not the real me. No one does except *him*, but to have my mind go there causes me to shake violently, bringing back the memories of the most horrific event of my life—the event that has altered my life forever. And to think, I'm not even a young girl, but a mature woman in her mid-thirties whose entire adult life has been a struggle to get through. This is not how it should've been.

I find the only things that even come close to keeping me sane is my remaining family and my journals. Since the day that *"It"* happened, the only thing that has helped me maintain my sanity is writing things down – my thoughts, dreams, nightmares, and fantasies – they all go into my journals. I keep them separate and color-coded by subjects because I might not write in one for months, then a thought or dream comes my way and I need to write it down. Each color reflects my different thoughts. The journals that I find myself consistently going to are the Fuchsia, for past memories, Blue for the present where I write of time and revenge, and then Orange for the future, and exploring me.

The two that get the most use are the blue and orange journals. My mind has shifted to a darker way of thinking now so most of my conscious time is spent in either a revenge or sexual mode, which is so not like the girl from my past, but she died that day so she could survive. I can't bring her back, and believe me, I've tried for years.

I've even spoken to counselors and therapists, but nothing has ever worked, so she's remained buried deep. Therefore, a new Quinn was born. I became a woman who lacked emotions or feelings, and that applies to everyone but my family and very few, close friends. All I did was get through each day the best I could.

I found that sex was one way to relieve some of the stresses in my life. It started with my many battery operated toys, then I progressed to having sex with a partner and found that I really enjoyed it, but I never made a connection with any of the men I slept with. They're just a means to an end.

My life isn't my own any longer, but maybe it never was. My journals have become a roadmap to my sanity, or lack of. This is my story.

CHAPTER 1

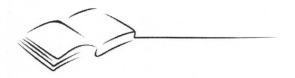

As I head to work on this fucking depressing, rainy Wednesday, traffic is again a bitch. I lift the coffee cup to my lips, blowing lightly on the hot liquid before taking a much-needed sip. This is definitely the nectar of the Gods.

Toying with the cup's lid, I vaguely listen to the radio as the two DJ's go back and forth with some shit about second dates, and how they want to know why someone wouldn't get a call for one. I laugh out loud because this is what is pissing people off nowadays. Really?

Once I stop laughing, I sit and really consider how fucked up my life is. I have no one. I mean, I do have family, but none that are close by, which is by choice. In my mind, I do it to keep them safe. I have very few friends and a very boring life, and here are people talking about stupid shit like a second date. "Get a fucking life, you losers," I scream at my car radio before I start to laugh again at the stupidity of the show itself.

Turning the corner heading toward the bakery, I look in my rearview mirror and swear that the car behind me in the left hand lane has been following me since I left my house. I start to sweat as my imagination runs away from me. My hands tighten on the steering wheel as I feel my heart beating, as if it's trying to jump out of my chest.

Son of a bitch, not another anxiety attack. This will make the third one this week. Trying to take a deep breath, I flip on my turn signal so I can park on the side street. As I get into a spot, I go to shift into park and glance back, only to see the black sports car coming over into the right lane, like it's going to pull over too.

Freaking out and not thinking, I fling the door open and get out, just as the car speeds by me. Due to the tinted windows, I can't see in but I'm able to see a part of the license plate that says STONE-something. Getting back in my car, I lock the doors and just sit there, trying to breathe. These anxiety attacks are getting worse and I know deep down that it's time, yet again, to speak to a professional or maybe get on some medication. For some reason, I can't let go of that night, and I probably never will. No matter how much time passes, when it feels like my life is finally going in a positive direction, something triggers a memory and it all comes back. He's still out there somewhere, and I know I may never be safe as long as he lives.

I work to pull myself together and finally shake it off. When I know I'm as good as I'm gonna get, I continue on my way to work, knowing we have a full day ahead of us.

The one thing that I love to do is bake. Since I was a little girl, my mom and grandma taught my sisters and me all the secrets to baking. They had recipes handed down from their mothers and grandmothers. After years of searching for something to do with my life, as job after job never panned out, I put it all on the line to open up a bakery, naming it Sweet Bits and Pieces. Never in my wildest dreams did I think it would take off as it did. I work in the back, doing most of the baking and decorating while my business partner and closest friend, Ivy, takes care of the front, doing the selling and advertising. It works great for the both of us.

As I pull my Jeep into my parking spot, the feeling returns. Looking back in the mirror, I see an SUV parked in the lot next to ours. I have no idea if it was there before I pulled in or not since my thoughts are still on the sports car.

Taking a deep breath, I reach into the glove box for my can of mace, gather my things, and get out of my Wrangler. I head toward the back entrance of my shop and just as I reach for the handle, I hear someone clear their throat behind me.

Turning around quickly, there's a man standing about five feet away from me. I reach into my coat pocket to get the can of mace, not taking my eyes off him as absolute terror starts to build in my body. It's him. Holy shit, he's found me.

I reach with my other hand for the door handle again, and that's when he makes his move, grabbing me by my arms and squeezing them tight. The panic takes over as my stomach clenches.

"Quinn, I've been looking for you for a long time, dear sister."

I look into the eyes of my brother, whom I haven't spoken to in years, and for good reason. He's the one *thing* I've worked so hard to hide from and for fuck's sake, he's finally found me.

Why did he have to look for me? After that night, I considered him dead and gone but here he is, looking perfectly healthy while our parents are rotting in their graves because of him. My sisters have spent years hiding out at the ranch from him, and let's not forget the shit he did to me.

18

"What the hell do you want? Why are you even here?" I'm not gonna lie, I'm scared. He is my worst nightmare come true and now he's here, making me look at the face that broke my world completely.

He grins that evil as shit grin, licks his lips and spews out, "You have something that belongs to me and I'm here to collect it. Once I have it, I'll leave you alone and never come knocking on your door again. Where's Dad's laptop, Quinn? I need it now, so cut the shit and quit wasting my time. Tell me where I can find it."

Shaking my head, I feel an uncontrollable laugh come from deep within. "Really? You're such a stupid asshole to think that after all this time and everything you've done that I would just give you what you want. You're out of your mind, you sick fuck."

He shakes his head and starts to reach behind his back, and with one arm now free, I pull the mace out of my pocket that I've been holding onto, and spray him dead in the face. I immediately grab the door handle to the bakery and rush inside, locking the door behind me as I start to scream out orders to my morning staff to lock the front door and get in the employee lounge immediately.

I make my way down the hall and grab the phone, dialing 911. I wait impatiently for the dispatcher to answer and when he does, I quickly rattle off the restraining order number on file, which I have memorized, and inform him that it's being violated and this person is also wanted for murder. He tells me to stay calm and that he's sending some units out right away. "Fuck, you want me to stay calm? This is the person responsible for my parent's murder and my torture. Calm isn't in my vocabulary at this point."

He tries reassuring me before I hang up, and now all I can do is wait for the police to show.

CHAPTER 2

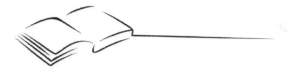

After the police arrive and search the area, they have no luck in finding my brother, leaving me a card in case he comes back. "Well thanks for nothing, you assholes. I may be too dead to make that call next time," I say as they walk out the door. I'm losing what little control I have on my emotions, but I know I need to pull my shit together.

Walking into the employee lounge, I give a brief explanation to my employees about what took place and tell them all to be extra careful and not to leave alone. This irks me, as I don't like sharing anything personal with anyone. Passing around a printed photo of his face from the security cameras, I then explain that he's dangerous, and if they see him to call the police immediately.

After a few questions, which I don't fully answer as it's none of their fucking business, they all get back to work.

I head to my office, sit down, and place my head in my hands. Was that him following me in the sports car? For some reason I don't think so because he was here when I pulled in. The timeframe isn't right. So I have that piece of shit snooping around, as well as someone following me on top of it. What the fuck? There's nothing like living life, looking over my shoulder every second of the day, waiting for shit to just come crashing down on me. However, it's what has to be done.

Knowing I have to get my head out of my ass and get some work done, I start going through the daily orders, then move on to the supply orders. This takes some time as we're getting into our busy season. I want to make sure we have everything, including the correct supplies on order. Yeah that's me, OCD to the max.

A knock on my door has me call out, "Come in." The door opens and in walks my business partner, but also one of my only friends, with two cups of steaming coffee.

"God, Ivy, you're a life saver. This is just what I need." I reach for the cup as she falls into the oversized chair to the left of my desk.

"What's going on, Quinn? I've never seen you so frazzled so tell me, who was that guy and why did you freak out? I can't help you if you don't tell me what's going on. You've always keep everything inside and I'm right here for you. Are we in danger?"

I place both hands on my desk, taking deep breaths. The time has come for me to tell her about my past because unfortunately, it's now bleeding into my present. "I've told no one what I'm about to tell you. The only people who know about this part of my life are the police and the multiple therapists I've seen over the years. I'm trusting you,

Ivy, with a part of me that I've tried to bury for so many years. I don't even know where to begin."

"Start at the beginning. I'm not going anywhere so just take your time. I have your back."

I pull my dark auburn hair back into a ponytail and walk to the couch in my office, patting the seat next to me. Ivy walks over with her coffee and sits in the corner, folding her legs underneath her. I'm amazed that we're friends, let alone business partners. She's the exact opposite of me outgoing and friendly with her long blonde hair and an ass most men, and women, envy. Even her tits are real. *Bitch.* Her best features though are her metallic grey eyes that I swear can see into your soul, which is what she's doing right now as she waits patiently, trying to get a peek into mine.

"There's some shit in my past that's horrific. It happened years ago and I've been running from it ever since. I don't even know how to explain it but I'll try. I come from what I thought was a normal family.

My parents loved each other and us, which were three girls and a boy. Raven's the oldest, then me, followed by my brother, then finally Viola. As time went on, we all knew something wasn't right with my brother, Walker. Even as a child, he was mean and cruel. The things he did to the neighborhood strays still makes my skin crawl to this day. As he got older, he stayed in trouble. My parents even took him to a professional. I believe he was around fifteen at the time. He beat the counselor almost to death because he didn't like the questions he was being asked. After the attack, the courts deemed him not suitable or safe to live with us. They placed him in a special hospital that was supposed to help him with his issues. I'm not sure what they did exactly, but his issues only seemed to get worse. He became anti-social and didn't want to see any of us. For years we tried until we all gave up, except my sister Raven. She continued to visit. Sometimes he'd see her, and other times he'd refuse her. This always bothered me, but I never felt comfortable asking her why she would want to stay in contact with him after what he did to our family.

Finally, after seven years, he was released – deemed cured and normal – whatever that term meant to them. Mom and Dad were so happy to have their son back in the family that they let him stay with them until he could get situated. He seemed to be doing well. He'd even gotten a job and never missed a day of work. Mom said he always helped my dad around the house and never complained about anything. This lasted for about a year or so, but my sisters and I started to worry. Walker never moved out and started acting as if he was doing my parents a favor by letting them live in their own home. Then we noticed a change in our parents, which Viola made us aware of since she still lived at home. They were getting up there in age, but they started to look like they were confused and withdrawn, which was definitely not like our parents.
The worse they got, the happier my brother appeared. He was relishing in their

diminishing health and mental well-being. It was like he got off on it or some sick shit.

One day I was coming down the stairs after cleaning their bathroom and heard Walker screaming at my mother. He was swearing and banging shit around, so I walked in and couldn't believe my eyes. My mom was on the floor, holding her side as he kicked her repeatedly. I jumped in front of her and shoved at him as hard as I could. He laughed and told me to get out of the way because he wasn't done with her yet. I remember screaming as my sisters came into the room. Raven walked over to Walker and whispered something in his ear that made him look at us, huddled by our mother. He said that it wasn't over yet and that every one of us would pay for getting in his business—that payback was a fucking bitch, right before he stormed out of the house. Raven actually tried to follow him until I screamed for her to help us with Mom. My dad, even in his withdrawn state, walked in, saw my mom on the floor, and called 911.

The police started an investigation into Walker and the shit hit the fan. It turned out that he was involved with some shady characters and needed a large amount of money. He was shaking our mom down for it because he thought she was easier than Dad was but she refused to help him, yet again, because she'd already bailed Walker out numerous times, unbeknownst to Dad. But the biggest shocker was when my parents informed my sisters and me that Walker was adopted. He was actually our cousin; his father was my dad's brother."

Taking a much-needed break, I drink down some cold coffee and close my eyes, trying to find the nerve to continue. Once I feel that I've got it, I go on, "They adopted him because my dad's brother was a psychopath. He'd gotten a prostitute with a bad drug habit pregnant and she died during childbirth. My uncle didn't want him so my parents stepped up and adopted him, raising him as their own. My parents prayed that Walker wouldn't get the sickness his father had or have any effects from the drugs his mother took while pregnant, but as he grew, they witnessed all the shit he did and knew he wasn't right, and that he probably never would be. They tried. They never gave up on him.

The police broke it down for us. He was a suspect in multiple rapes and abductions. He hung out with a bunch of guys who were getting away with their crimes because no one would press charges against them. The police suggested the order of protection and my dad agreed.

As time went on, we were careful, but Walker never showed his face. My parents recovered from Walker's abuse after we discovered that he was drugging them. To try and start fresh, they went as far as selling their house and moving to the next town over. Raven and I decided to go with them so we sold our places too. We got comfortable and after so much time with nothing happening, we let our guard down. That's when Walker came back into our lives."

I stretch my back and walk around to my desk. I sit down in the chair while avoiding Ivy's stare as I unlock the top drawer and pull out a file, placing it on the corner of my desk. "Don't look yet. Let me explain what happened before you look through that." Ivy pulls a chair over and sits as she waits patiently.

"It was early fall when we finally heard from Walker. He showed up, asking to come in and visit—to catch up. When my parents told him no, he then invited us to come to his place. He said that he needed to show us how he was turning his life around and how much he'd changed. Raven and Viola were uneasy and skeptical, just as I was, but my parents being the kind, loving, and naive people they were, agreed. They made plans of when, where and a time. After he left, my sister Viola asked if we should tell the police that Walker was there, as the order of protection had been continued over the years. My mom just shook her head and said no, that he was our Walker and she believed him. She believed that he had changed and wouldn't do anything to hurt us because before, he was confused, but now he seemed to be on the right track. He said that he was getting help, so Mom assumed he was getting better with counseling and medication, and that he deserved a second chance. I looked at my mother like she was nuts. He'd beaten her so bad that day that she walked with a permanent limp.

I've never forgotten that day, nor had I forgotten the look in Walker's eyes. He enjoyed seeing her in pain, watching her suffer. I saw a sadist for the first time, up close and personal. He was coming from some deep, dark place and I knew that something had snapped that night. I didn't want to go, but the next evening we all headed over to Walker's place, and what happened that night altered our lives forever.

CHAPTER 3

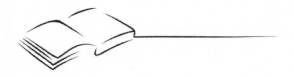

"Quinn, you have to let it out. Whatever it is, it's killing you slowly. I see it every day, but I never pry into your personal business. You're always hiding and looking over your shoulder like someone's coming for you, so whatever this is, you shouldn't have to carry it yourself. You have me, and I'm willing to help you carry it, if you'll let me."

Squeezing her hand, I nod my head in agreement. I can tell that she's getting nervous about hearing the rest, so I want to get it out as quick as possible for both our sakes.

"I had a feeling something was off so before we left, I went into the garage and got my dad's camping knife, then went into their bedroom and found the gun that Dad hid in the closet in a box. Finally, I went into the junk drawer in the kitchen and pulled out the can of Mace. I put the camping knife in my hoodie pocket, the gun in the back of my pants, and the Mace in my sock, under my jeans. I've always listened to my gut, and it was telling me that I needed to protect myself. And since my parents wouldn't listen to us, I felt like I had no choice.

We took two cars because Raven was supposed to work later that night. Walker told us that he was living with a friend in a loft, so when we found the address on the building, we didn't think twice because it was so big, and lofts are big, right? It wasn't in the best part of town, but it wasn't the worst, either.

Mom had stayed up all night cooking and baking, so her arms were filled with containers for Walker. Dad rang the bell and Walker appeared immediately, like he was just standing at the door waiting for us. He hurried us in, looking up and down the street before slamming the door closed.

33

Viola turned her head, looking at me with dread in her eyes. We both felt it; an ominous feeling of something bad in the air—something *wrong*. Trying to back up toward the door we just entered, I felt a hand at my back. I screamed and turned to see a guy looking down at me. He was tall, over six feet tall, and he scared the shit out of me. He purposely pushed me forward until I saw what my family was looking at in horror. This wasn't a loft or an apartment. This was an abandoned warehouse, set up for something so sick and twisted that my mind couldn't even wrap around what I was seeing. There were gurneys with chains attached to them. Beside each gurney, there was a table with instruments peeking through the coverings. I looked over and saw a scalpel next to some sort of pliers. I mean, what the fuck had we just walked into? I would've sworn my mind was playing tricks on me and that it was some sick joke, but the look on my family's faces showed me that it wasn't just me. They were scared shitless too.

We were all staring at Walker while he grinned like a fuckin' maniac, reminding me of when he told us that we would all eventually pay. My dad started to speak but Walker slammed his fist into his jaw. We started screaming and I ran to him, just as a couple more guys came in and at that precise moment, I knew that we weren't getting out of there alive.

I had to do something, or at least try, so I charged toward Walker, yelling for the girls to get the fuck out and go get help. I obviously caught the guys off guard, giving Raven and Viola time to run for the front door and get out just as I jumped on Walker, bringing him down with me as I clawed at him with my nails. While he was trying to get control of me, I pulled my knee up and connected with his groin as hard as I could, giving me the chance to grab the knife in my hoodie and stab the guy who was trying to hold me from behind. When he let go, howling in pain, I crawled toward my mom who couldn't have ran with the girls to get out of there even if she'd tried.

Walker grabbed a huge knife and yanked my mom by the neck before I could get to her. Ivy, the fear in her eyes broke my fucking heart. She knew that things weren't going to end well. She gave me a look that I will never forget as long as my feet remain on this earth. They were filled with so much love, sorrow, and regret as she mouthed the words that torn my heart out "I'm so sorry Quinn" and all I could do was smile back, trying to relay all of it back to her.

My dad was still on the ground, trying to get his bearings when I asked Walker why. I couldn't understand why he hated us so much when all we did was love and help him, and what he said made me sick. He said that he'd thought of nothing else but that moment since the day he walked out of our home. With them dead, the life insurance money would go to us kids, and he figured that he could manipulate us into giving our shares to him because he needed that money, and he'd do anything to get it. That was when Dad told him that he and

Mom changed the beneficiaries on the life insurance policies after he went crazy and attacked Mom, leaving everything to us girls.

When Walker heard that, he raised the knife and slammed it deep into my mom's chest. He killed her, Ivy. He stabbed the woman who raised and loved him as her own and he didn't give a fuck. I had to watch Mom die. It happened so fast that I had no time to react. I couldn't do anything to help her."

I can't stop the tears from falling when I remember the look on her face as she died. I didn't save her. I don't know what I expected to happen, but I should've done something, I just don't know what, no matter how many times I go over it.

"He pulled the knife out and started walking toward Dad. Even in shock, I pulled the gun from my pants and pointed it at Walker, shooting him in the shoulder. What happened next happened so fast that I'm not sure what to describe first. I saw one of the guys raise his own gun, aiming it at my dad so I didn't even think. I aimed and shot, hitting him right in the head and that's truly when all hell broke loose. They started pulling guns and knives out, going straight for my dad. He was trying to get to this metal pipe lying on the ground but they were like rabid dogs. They beat him to death, even as I emptied the gun at them, trying not to hit my dad in the process. I hit a couple of them, but it didn't slow the rest of them down. A few of the guys came at me and tackled me to the floor, but they didn't beat me. There I was, just having watched my mom and dad get murdered right in front of me and I knew that I would be next. My mind had no way to comprehend the sheer evil I was about to face. Death would have been better."

I take a shaky breath, wishing that I'd never started this conversation, but I also knew that I couldn't stop now. Ivy has sat here, listening to it all with tears streaming down her cheeks. I shouldn't have put this on her, but I need to tell her the rest.

"They tied me to one of the gurneys and they all took turns raping me, all more than once, amongst other things they did to me to get off. It went on for what felt like days when it was only hours, but enough time to do plenty of damage with time to spare. The things they put me through are etched in my mind forever. Even Walker, after everything they did to me, moved the gurney closer to the sink and with a hose, sprayed me down with ice-cold water until he sprayed off what the others left on and in me, and then he took his turn. He untied me and shoved me off the gurney, onto the floor. He sodomized me brutally. I had never had anal sex before, and he tore me up. The way he took me was so painful that I must have passed out because I woke up being slapped across the face. Walker was lying over me, raping me again, telling me that this would go on 'til my sisters finally brought help. He apparently had a lookout, waiting for anyone to show up so they could get out fast after he finished me off. Once Walker finished, a guy brought over a long iron. I was in so much pain that I didn't understand what he was planning to do with it until I felt the burn. The iron was red-hot and being pressed into my inner thigh. Walker looked at me with a deranged smile as I screamed, not having much of a voice left. I later realized that he had branded me with a W, and the number 13. There were other women out there with the letter W and other numbers branded on them I found out later.

I lost consciousness a few times but he woke me up every time by slapping my face repeatedly. Seeing the pain I was in turned him on so he decided to do other things to me that included using my mouth, and then he passed me off to let the others continue their assaults on me two, even three at a time. I was violated in every way you could possibly imagine. Anything went with them, and I mean anything.

I'd given up on my sisters ever bringing help. I mean, how could they get away and not find help? No one was coming.

My mind started to shut down. I blocked out a lot after what my brother did and just lied there, letting them do whatever they wanted. I do remember that I prayed for death. I even asked them for it, but they just laughed and went on with what they were doing.

At one point I locked onto a pair of the deepest emerald green eyes I'd ever seen. He was at the windows, watching everything they were doing to me. I was confused when I saw that he had tears running down his face. Not knowing who he was I was so fucking confused as to why he didn't just go get help? Why stand there and watch me being brutalized and do absolutely nothing. When I would go to turn my head, he'd tap softly on the window, shaking his head and pointing to his eyes, then mine. I guessed that he was trying to give me something to focus on, but I never understood why he just stood there. I was torn because part of me felt like I

41

appreciated what he was trying to do but hated him for doing nothing at the same time. But the other part of me just hated him and couldn't believe he thought he was helping me. I didn't need his pity. I needed his fucking help."

Grabbing a bottle of water off my desk, I gulp it down as my body trembles and tears spill out. I'm not an emotional person, but once they start, I can't stop them. I'd made it through the whole story and now I'm a fucking mess as I grab for the garbage can and throw up.

Ivy stands by me, rubbing up and down my back saying nothing, which to me says volumes, and I appreciate it. What do you say to a story like that?

When I'm finally done, she tries to put on a strong front for me, and she has no idea what that means to me.

"I'm stunned and disgusted, Quinn. I can never begin to understand what you went through and I won't pretend to, but I'll help you in any way that I can." She hesitates, like she needs to say something

else so I nod, telling her to just say it. "I'm
not trying to upset you, but I have to ask.
What happened to your sisters? Why didn't
they bring help?"

"When I finally came to, I was in the
hospital, surrounded by my sisters and the
police who had finally found me. When they
ran out of the loft, one of Walker's friends
followed them so they had to find
somewhere to hide. They ended up in an
abandoned warehouse a couple of blocks
down while the guy searched the building
for them. They were lucky and found a place
to hide, under a portion of flooring. When he
finally left, they busted ass to the nearest
police station but by then, so much time had
gone by and they were having a hard time
remembering where the building we were at
was.

The cops, with Raven and Viola's
help, finally found their way to the loft.
Unfortunately, so much time had gone by
that Walker and his friends were gone when
they arrived. My sisters walked in to see our
parents' dead, along with a few guys that I

43

was able to shoot. Then there was me. From what they told me, I was pretty close to death myself with the beatings I'd taken throughout the night." Taking a breath, I finish up, "It's been years, and lots of relocations in different cities and towns to try and stay away from Walker, but all of it's been for nothing. He's found me, and I have nowhere else to go." Realizing at that moment if he's located me, what's to stop him from finding Raven and Viola. Shit. If he finds them, he'll find out my secret. I can't let that happen. I've got to protect them no matter what.

After Ivy sees what's in the file on my desk, she reaches down and hugs me tight. For the first time in years, someone is giving *me* support. It tears at my heart as I start to truly cry for the first time in ages, sobbing uncontrollably. Ivy just holds me tighter, letting me get it all out. It's almost cathartic—like a cleansing or something. I hug her back, knowing that my life is going down a horrible path again, and it's all because of that bastard Walker.

CHAPTER 4

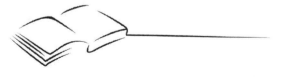

After sharing my horrible and brutal past with Ivy, we try to get back to normal, mostly for the staff. I, as usual, stay in the back, baking and decorating as Ivy and the rest of my small staff handle the customers. Thank God time flies by because my mind is shifting all over the place. I can't keep everything together much longer. Actually, I can't believe that for the first time in a long time, I had to re-frost a birthday cake due to my mind not being on my job and fucking it up.

I close up so we can do our usual cleanup and prep for the morning rush. Once we finish, we all head out together to an early evening that's muggy, and I can smell a storm on the horizon.

"Quinn, do you want me to come home with you and stay the night? Or you can come to my place and we can keep each other company. We could sit around in our PJ's and pig out on junk food," she finishes with a grin.

"No, Ivy, but thank you for the offer. I'm going home to chill, maybe have a drink and just veg out with the security system on. I feel better letting all that shit out today, but I feel bad that now you have it in your head."

She grabs and pulls me in for another one of her tight hugs. "I'm glad that you trusted me enough to share it with me. Love ya girl—always will. If you need me just call me, promise?" I shake my head as she turns and heads to her car.

I lied. I'm not ok. I drive home feeling like my body is on the verge of a physical and mental breakdown. I'm trying to decide if I should call Raven and Viola or leave them out of this shit. They have enough on their plates with their own pain from that night and the secret that they are taking care of for me. Walker can never find out what happened after that night because in his sick, twisted mind, the games would just continue, as he would have something else to hold over my head and use to get what he wants.

Driving slowly down my dead end street, I don't see anything out of the ordinary as I pull into my driveway. Grabbing all my stuff, including the extra can of mace stored under my seat, I open the door and look back down the road. That's when I see a sports car making its way down the road. I slam my door closed and rush to the front door, keys at the ready when I hear a car door slam and the sound of feet running on concrete. Distracted and scared as hell, I drop my keys on the porch. Bending to pick them up, I glance back and my breath catches in my throat.

As scared as I am, my mouth drops open. Holy shit! I see the hottest man ever running up my driveway. He has on a baseball hat that's pulled low over his eyes while his wavy brown hair is barely contained in his hat. It takes me only seconds to see these things. I'm trying to catch my breath while picking up my keys, ignoring him as I go to open my front door.

Suddenly he's right here, moving me away from my door and taking my keys. Before I can scream, his hand is over my mouth, whispering in my ear, "Stay here, Quinn. Don't move until I come back out and get ya, ya hear?"

I can't control my body as it begins convulsing uncontrollably for the second time today. What was I thinking coming home?

I nod, having not only dropped my keys, but everything else, including the mace. This mystery man opens my door, reaching for a gun in the back of his jeans and enters the code to turn my alarm off. What the fuck? I look around and find my mace, stuffing it and my hand in my pocket, ready to use it if I need to. I wait and stare at my front door. I don't know why. He's not setting off any warning bells and he carries himself almost in a professional way, like he's a cop or something, but who the fuck is he and how does he know my name? The longer I wait, the more freaked out I feel. Today is one of those days where you just want a do-over.

A couple of minutes later, the door opens and he steps out. He reaches down to grab my hand but I pull out of his reach as he tells me, "All clear."

I move around him to enter my home and unfortunately, he follows. "I don't know who you are but get the hell out of my house before I call the police."

Moving my eyes up his torso to his face, I feel the air leave my lungs as I look into a set of piercing green eyes. As I feel the room begin to spin and start to see stars, I hear him yelling, "Quinn, breathe. Son of a bitch, take a deep breath, woman."

I do. I sucked in a deep breath, not even realizing I've been holding it. I feel disoriented so I sit down and get my shit together. Once I feel better, I'm afraid to look up to see if it really is him, so I sit still and remain quiet.

He bends down in front of me and lifts my face gently so I'm looking directly into those striking green eyes as he stares at me inquisitively. I feel as if we're having a battle of wills as we continue to stare at each other. Finally his eyes leave mine to flow over my face, down my body and back to my eyes again.

I cannot take a minute more of this. My day from hell just continues to get worse. "Who the fuck are you and what do you want? Didn't you see enough of me back then because not much has changed Asshole?" I can feel my armor crashing up around me.

His mouth begins twitching as he looks at me. I'm not finding a fucking thing funny about this situation, especially since *he* watched every horrible thing that happened to me that night. I start to get pissed, but before I can do or say anything, he finally speaks. "Quinn, please calm down and don't go losin' your shit. I'm gonna explain who I am and what the fuck is goin' on. Just take a deep breath and listen, ok?" Giving him a brief nod, he continues, "I know from the way you're looking at me that you recognize me, am I right?" Once again I nod, "Dammit. Before I go any further, you have to believe if I could have done something back then, I would have. You have no idea how that day has haunted me over the years.

"Haunted you? Seriously? *I'm* the one who had to live through it all, not sit at some fucking window watching it happen and not doing a goddamn thing to stop it." I scream in his face.

"Let me try to explain this to you. Shit, you don't even know who I am, do you? My name is Stone Myanto and Walker was my friend back then. Don't you remember me at all?"

At his words I'm ready to bolt, but again he grabs my hands, keeping me in place. "His dad is your uncle who was a serious psychopath. Your dad kept a close

eye on your uncle when he was incarcerated to see if he ever reached out to Walker. I spoke to your father about Walker quite a few times, but he didn't want to believe that Walker could be such a horrible person."
Wait did I hear him correctly?

"You spoke to my father? When?"

Stone takes a deep breath as he pulls his hands away from mine. Standing up, he walks toward my kitchen, "Come on, Quinn. Let's get some coffee 'cause this is gonna take a while. Are you ready?"
Standing up, I follow him with all kinds of questions in my head. What's happening, and why, after all this time, does he finally come to me?

CHAPTER 5

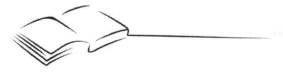

We're sitting at the kitchen table, each of us holding a cup of freshly brewed coffee. Stone looks slightly nervous as I wait for him to explain what he came here for. He truly is sexy. His features look to be carved out of stone and the depth of green in his eyes is breathtaking. Not since I saw them the first time that night have I ever seen eyes this green. Once he takes his hat off, his hair looks messy, and I can't help but like it.

"Quinn, your dad and Walker's had a really rough upbringing. Their old man was a drunk, and a mean one at that from the way your dad talked." My eyes shoot to his in shock. He definitely knew something about my dad. "The difference is your dad took that and used it to become a better man while Walker's dad, Marty, used it as an excuse to be one mean son of a bitch. Do you know what your dad did for a living?"

"Actually, no, I don't exactly know. He never spoke about it. All we knew was that he worked in an office and traveled here and there. Why, are you going to tell me he was FBI or CIA, because I won't believe it? There's no way."

Stone reaches into his back pocket, pulling his wallet out and tossing a card my way. Glancing down, I'm shocked to see an ID card with my dad's picture on it.

"Your dad did work for the government in a top-secret specialized area, dealing with environmental issues. He was a genius and was in the process of getting one of his programs patented that would assist people everywhere to have clean drinking water. It's what got him killed. Marty and Walker wanted that program. Marty had many contacts that would pay him huge amounts of cash to keep that off the grid. Do you get what I'm saying?

Walker's dad had connections that didn't want your dad to succeed with his work. Now, who do you think that would have been, because I have a real good idea."

"My dad wouldn't let something, even as important as that, come between our family. So, what am I missing?" Something was off and I could feel deep down that Stone was leaving something out and I didn't know why.

"Your dad had been working with the government to shut down your uncle. Even being in jail didn't keep him out of the loop and what he was into wasn't good. So besides working on his lifelong dream of helping people less fortunate than most, your dad was assisting the government in bringing your uncle and his partners down. Between drugs, pimping, trafficking, and everything in between, the world would be a better place without them in it. Your dad was gathering information from each visit with your Uncle Marty. The problem was that Marty's reach was greater than anyone could imagine. He was an evil man. Your uncle is the one who gave Walker the information that changed your families' lives that night. He let Walker loose that night knowing fully the extent his son would go to."

"So, why are you and Walker suddenly back in my life? What's changed? Seeing Walker today and having you here is like a slap in the face, bringing up all the shit I've been trying to forget. I need to know because I'm about to lose my fucking mind." I drop my head into my hands as my eyes start to fill up with tears. I can't do this again. I have too much to lose now and I will not let anyone know my secrets, definitely not Stone, and especially not Walker.

"I'm not finished yet, so let me get this out. Obviously you don't know that Your Uncle Marty died three weeks ago and his criminal empire is falling apart. Walker's trying to get control and hold it together but he isn't his dad and the people involved don't trust him. They haven't forgotten how he handled that shit with you and your family." Taking a drink of his coffee and rubbing his eyes, he pushes forward, "Your uncle couldn't find any of you until right before his death. He wanted that laptop. I'm not sure why, but we assume it's for your father's notes. Marty convinced Walker during the last couple weeks of his life to make sure he got that computer from you, no matter what. That's why, after all these years, Walker approached you. With his dad gone, shit's hittin' the fan in their criminal world. He needs to get his hands on that laptop to see what your dad had on there. Marty was convinced that everything your dad had worked on was on his laptop, including the conversations he had with Marty from their prior meetings in jail and now Walker needs it."

"That's all good and dandy, but what makes everyone think I have the laptop after all these years?"

Stone glances my way then drops his head. "Raven told Walker you had it when he spoke to her recently. We have it on tape."

Feeling the panic rise in my chest, I jump up and run to grab my phone. Hands shaking, I try to dial the ranch's number but drop the fucking phone. Reaching to pick it up, I once again feel his presence behind me. Grabbing the phone from me, he hangs it up and guides me back to my chair. "Don't bother calling her. They're not there anymore."

I actually hear the panic in my voice, "What do you mean *they* aren't there? Where in the hell are my sisters if they aren't at the ranch?"

"I've been your security for years now. You have no secrets, do you get me?" Hearing this, my head jerks up and my eyes go wide. "Yeah, you get me. I was following your family that night to make sure you were safe and we see how well that turned out. I know you have a ton of questions, but let me break this down as simple as possible. Yes, I was there that night we both know that. What you don't know is that I called it in to my boss and no, no one came. After no one showed, I went to put in another call for help and my fucking cell was dead. I didn't feel comfortable leaving you so instead, I stayed outside that window and tried to give you what I could. You had me there with you and don't think that shit hasn't fucked me up 'cause it has. By the time I got it in my head to leave you and go find help, the girls came back. I thank God every day that even though they were fuckin' late, Raven and Viola were able to bring help and save your life—something I failed to do because I trusted the wrong person as back-up. Just so you know, I eventually took my boss down and he's now spending time in jail. I found out that he was working with your Uncle Marty.

Since that day, I've been watching your back so I know your secret, or should I say, *"secrets."* You don't have to worry though. They're safe with me darlin', I promise you that."

"Get the fuck out of my house now. I'm not playing. I don't want to hear anything more from you so GET OUT!" As I start to lose my shit, he pulls me to him. I feel his body heat seeping into me, calming me.

"Sugar, ain't goin' anywhere so calm down. We need to get past all this so we can figure out what needs to be done next, so please, I just need you to calm down so we can think."

Never since that night have I been in the arms of a man for just comfort. He wraps himself around me like he's protecting me and for a split second, it actually feels really nice to let another human being hold me, of the male persuasion, that is.

Then my head starts to get back in the game. I can't trust this son of a bitch—I don't even know him. This sounds like a made up story if I ever heard one. I have no idea who the hell he is, and I need to get back to figuring out how to handle Walker.

"Thanks for the information. Once I get this shit with Walker straightened out, we'll go over all you've shared, but right now, I need you to go so I can handle my personal and family business."

CHAPTER 6

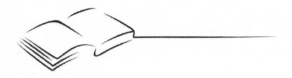

Shit, what part of this doesn't she get? I've spent most of my adult life watching her, trying to keep all that evil away from her and her family. It hasn't been easy, staying a step ahead of Marty and Walker with my small crew. Quinn doesn't realize that night changed my life. At one time I was heading in a similar path as Walker, but after witnessing the horrors that was Walker growing up, I swore to myself to get my shit together and I had been going down a different path that included working with people who wanted to take Walker down.

I work for a special division of the government, same as Quinn's dad did, except I'm one of the elite used for protection. We are always training for anything and everything. Quinn doesn't even know how many people admired her father and still do. Watching her trying to hold it together, I know that my decision to change the course of my life which eventually led to protecting her was the right one.

I look up to see her leaving the room, heading to her bedroom. I know the entire floor plan as I've been in here before. I set up surveillance in her small house and at the ranch where the rest of her family has been in hiding.

All these years, we've been waiting for Marty's Organization to make their move and they finally have. Sending Walker to confront Quinn was a mistake because it showed us that their organization was back in town and in full force to wreak havoc around this small community.

There have been missing women around the area recently, bodies have been turning up with the same brand Quinn has on her thigh with different numbers. We think this is Walker's way of letting us know how many women he has violated then killed. The last victim that I've heard about had the W with the number 31 burned into her upper thigh. Besides bodies, the drugs on the street seem heavier, so the assumption is that they're moving forward with their plans.

Realizing she's been gone for a while, I get up and walk down the hallway. Coming to her room on quiet feet, my eyes are drawn to her bed, which is empty. Then looking the room over and not seeing her, I walk in with the intention to check the bathroom out when I hear a slight movement to my left from behind the door.

I see her shadow behind me cast across her floor as her arm aims something toward me. Putting my hand over my head, I rush forward as she points that fuckin' can of mace at me and pushes the button. Her aim is off as the liquid only hits the corner of one eye, but that shit fuckin' burns.

Grabbing her arms, I twist as she drops the can with a scream of pain. I shove her toward the bed and I can actually feel her panic pulsing in the room. Needing to calm my own shit down, I push her forward as she falls on the bed, but I stay right where I am so she knows I don't mean to do her harm. She lands on her stomach and quickly turns to her back, pushing herself farther away on the bed. We both wait, watching to see who makes the next move.

Finally, I put my hands in the air, "I'm not the enemy here, I swear to God, darlin'. Take just a minute and think. Why would I go through all this fuckin' trouble to tell you everything if my only intention was to hurt you? You're a smart woman, so use that brain 'cause we're wastin' time. We need to finish our talk so I can tell you where your family is and then let you make the call to put your mind at ease. Will that work for you?"

I can already see that she's gonna be a fuckin' handful.

Listening to his calm voice, I try to relax and know he's right, so I nod and push myself to sit on the edge of the bed. Stone pulls the chair from the corner in front of me and sits. "So do you have any questions that I can try to answer for you?"

"Yeah, a ton, but right now I'm so confused and tired. Please just tell me my family is alright. That's the most important thing to me right now."

I watch him dial a number and wait for someone to answer. I can hear someone begin to speak on the other end of the line and he sounds like an idiot. Who uses the words *Yo*, and *Dude*? Stone asks for the man on the other end to give the phone to Raven and hands it over to me. "Talk to her so she can tell you that they're all ok."

"Raven, is that you? Are you ok? Is *everyone* ok?"

"We're all here and we're all fine, but who are these guys? What do they want?"

"Aunt Raven, is that mom? Tell her we're being good like she always tells us to be, but we're really hungry. Is she coming here too?"

Hearing my babies, my twin's voices, brings relief like nothing ever could. They're ok and hungry and for some reason, I start to laugh.

Stone takes the phone and tells Raven to give the phone back to someone named Johnny. He tells this Johnny to feed everyone and bed down for the night, and to call if they need anything.

Still laughing, I lay back on my bed and curl up in the fetal position. As I look around my room, the journals on the side table draw my attention. For years I've kept it all locked down tight—never letting my sisters or the twins know how bad it was or show them *me* when I would slowly fall apart. That was the purpose of the journals. Each counselor and therapist recommended that I do this, writing everything down as a form of getting it out when I didn't want to talk about it. So in the beginning, I did just that. Everything that I need to get out is written down. It's allowed me to live in this world and not have another nervous breakdown.

But as the years went on and the healing slowly started, my journaling came full circle. The only ones I continue to write in are the three at my bedside, separated by past, present, and future.

Moving toward the side of the bed, I reach for the journals just as Stone comes around and sits in that spot. He's watching me closely now. He beats me to them and I pounce, grabbing them and moving to the opposite end of the bed. "Don't even think of touching these. They're personal, private, and not for anyone else to see, let alone read. These have been my only way to survive what happened so don't touch them again."

He glances back and forth between the journals and me with a guilty expression when it suddenly hits me like a brick. I'm so fucking pissed that I leap up from the bed, hitting him with my free hand. "You asshole. Tell me you haven't read them. Tell me that you didn't violate my privacy."

When he doesn't answer, I know. "You are such a dick. Get the fuck out of my house now, you bastard," I scream as I jump from the bed and run to the bathroom, but I'm not fast enough. He grabs me around my waist and pulls me back into him.

My hands release the bundle of journals and they fall to the ground, opening at random pages. As Stone holds me close I can feel his cock start to get hard pressing against my ass and it just pisses me off even more. Struggling to break free, he tightens his grip with one hand as his other grabs my hair, jerking my head back. "Quinn, stop right now and let me explain this shit to you. Yes, I read them because I had to get a pulse on you and where you were at, not to get in your business." As soon as I feel his breath on my skin, my nipples harden. I'm pissed all over again that my body would respond to this stranger who has done nothing but piss me off and violate my privacy. It makes me sick but for some reason apparently horny too from the way my body is reacting. What the fuck is wrong with me?

I can tell the exact moment he feels my reaction as his hand starts to caress my stomach. He pushes his cock against my ass as he lines his body behind me. As pissed off as I am, the familiar heat starts to travel down my body to my core. I can't stop my response to him as I arch into him, feeling him thrust back against me as he lets out a long breath, telling me how affected he is too. At least I'm not the only one reacting like a sex-starved adolescent with a frigging stranger. A stranger who is a part of the worst time of my life.

It takes everything in me to push away from him and he lets me. I turn, coming face to face with him. I watch as his features turn to stone as tears run freely from my eyes. The knowledge of him reading my journals has brought me to my knees. I can feel an emotional breakdown coming. No one knows what goes on in my head. Not the therapists, not the police, and not even my family. I have plans that no one is supposed to know about. I've been plotting my revenge against every one of those assholes that not only took my parents from me, but took everything from me, just because they could. This is my private revenge, and now Stone has taken that from me.

My emotions are so raw at this moment. Having this man with all my personal information that I don't even know is enough to make me want to beat the shit out of him, but it's not only that. I'm somehow attracted to this man, and he's obviously attracted to me too.

So not over analyzing this moment and taking a huge risk being on emotional overload and feeling close to a breakdown and not wanting to be alone, I hesitantly raise my hand slowly to his face and caress his cheek. He leans into my hand, letting a sigh escape through his full lips. I know that I should be asking more questions, but don't because right now as confusing as it is I need to feel safe, comforted and grounded with all this shit happening. And to make this more of a cluster fuck, I want it from the man who has just appeared back in my life

71

again invading my mind and bringing up memories I didn't want, while he tried to explain his part in my life. Trying to comprehend Stone knowing so much about me was unnerving. There was a part of me that hated him because of the past and his part in it. But the other part of me, the damaged part needed to feel something, anything again with another human being. And for reasons unknown we had a connection and attraction that was hard to deny. So I looked him in the eyes and ask him, "please, will you stay and just hold me tonight?"

Looking intently for a minute he finally shakes his head as if to clear it.

"Quinn get out of those clothes, put on your PJ's and I'll be right back as I'm not goin' anywhere. I wanna check the house out. You hungry?"

As soon as he asks my stomach growls as my cheeks turn redder than an apple. Stone lets loose with a loud relieved laugh as the tension between us seems to lift slightly.

"Yeah, I guess I could eat. Take-out menus are in drawer by the stove." He turns and leaves as I grab some clothes and head to the bathroom to change.

CHAPTER 7

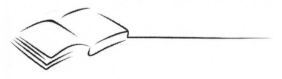

Feeling full, I continue to stuff Sesame Chicken into my mouth. Every now and then I look to see what Stone's doing. He, like me, is eating like he hasn't in days. The Mongolian Beef that's being shoved into his mouth looks good except for the flush on his face and neck from the heat of his entrée, letting me know without asking that it's spicy.

As I reach for my drink, Stone asks, "How you holding up, Sugar?"

I shake my head, indicating I'm not doing well. "What are we doing, Stone? Where do we go from here and are my children and sisters safe from our psycho cousin?"

He reaches across the table, grabbing my hand in his as he explains to me, "I promise you that nothing will happen to anyone you care about. My guys are the best and they're there now with Raven, Viola and the kids. Let's clean up and then we'll talk." Feeling slightly weird cleaning my kitchen with a man in it, I get over it and we get the job done. Then we head into the family room as I take one end of the couch and he takes the other so we face each other.

"Do you have the laptop, Quinn? I ask 'cause it all boils down to that computer and if you don't have it, we'll have to figure out another way to handle this situation. If you do have it, then we need to get it to a safe place that Walker won't be able to get his hands on it. Also thinking you might wanna take some time away from Sweet Bits & Pieces since he now knows where you work."

"I don't just work there. That's my bakery. I can't just walk away."

"How much do you trust Ivy?

"I trust her completely we're partners. Why?"

"How about instead of being in the bakery all day, we switch it up and you bake during the evening when we can watch you and Ivy handles the day-to-day shit. Would that work? You'd still be in the loop, so to speak, but still protected by either one of my boys or me. They'll be with you so Walker won't be able to get to you."

Thinking on his suggestion, I realize it could work. It really didn't matter if I baked at night or during the day, just as long as all the baked goods were there. Cakes and special orders would just be done sooner rather than later. It would actually run like it did in the beginning when I did work evenings so that when the twins were here, I was home with them. Those days were hell. Sleep was rare and I still thank all that's holy for Raven and Viola who were my only help with the babies.

"Yes, I can work with that. I'll have to speak with Ivy so she's aware of what's going on, but I doubt it will be a problem. She's had my back 100% from the start."

"Good. Now that that's settled, let's move on to the bigger issues. First we need to find out who sold you out to Walker. Someone did and it has to be someone close. I'm gonna need a list of everyone in your life. I already have my tech guy, Moose, looking into both Raven and Viola."

"What the fuck are you saying? Those are my sisters. Why would you investigate them?" Hearing the anger in my voice, he rocks back in his chair.

"Raven's been in touch with Walker on and off all these years. As far as we can tell, she never gave away any info on you or the twins, but it's still kinda strange that she would even want to talk to him after what he did to all of you, don't you think?"
His question is one that I've had for years, but I've been too chicken to ask her why. Raven has always been a bit different, no strange is a better word, where Viola and I are similar in our personalities. Sometimes it appeared as if Raven not only hated Walker,

but was scared to death of him. Then at other times, she always wanted to give him a second chance, which never made sense to me. I've seen the differences over the years and now I'm wondering if I made a mistake leaving and trusting her with my kids. The only reason my kids are with her is because of Viola. My kid sister would never let anyone or anything hurt her niece and nephew. She has even taken classes for self-defense so that she would be prepared for anything. Stone must be reading my mind.

"The kids are safe. No matter what Walker or Raven do or don't do, no one is getting those kids away from my guys. They're prepared to give their lives for those kids, so don't worry. They're safe."

This day feels like it's been a week wrapped into sixteen hours. "Well thank you for all you've done for me. I really do appreciate it. I know earlier I asked you to stay the night but that was in the moment after you explained everything to me and I was feeling emotional. I'm gonna take a shower and go to bed so if you want to take off, go ahead. We can meet up in the morning and go to the kids after I explain the situation to Ivy, ok?"

I get up to put the dishes in the dishwasher and Stone follows me. When I look at him, he actually scares me. "Are you kidding me? Do you really think I'm gonna leave you here alone? I'm gonna tell you the plan so there's no miscommunication. I'll be sleeping here tonight either on the couch or in your spare room. I'm not leaving you alone, so go take your shower and I'll clean this shit up."

"Take the couch. It's actually really comfy and besides, my spare bedroom doesn't have a bed. Use the spare bathroom though if you want a shower." Turning, I start to leave, but stop, "Thank you again, and I really mean it. Tonight could've been so much worse. You have no idea how much you being here will help me sleep tonight. You probably think I'm nuts stay, go, stay and I won't lie, I'm scared to death, but having you here gives me some peace and security. Goodnight Stone." I then head to my room to shower and go to sleep so I can forget this day ever happened.

CHAPTER 8

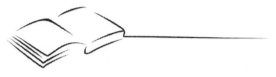

Hearing the screaming coming from Quinn's bedroom, I jump up from the couch, grab my Glock and run down the hall. Switching the light on, I take in the scene. Quinn's rocking back and forth in her bed, screaming through a nightmare. Seeing her like this after all these years tears my heart out. I want to be the one who squeezes out the last breath Walker ever takes with my bare hands.

Cautiously I approach the bed and without touching her, I start calling out her name. "Quinn, come on baby, wake up. You're having a bad dream." Finally her eyes slowly open and the intense pain in them take my breath away. Fuck. She's so beautiful I think to myself as I try to reign in my hard-on so I don't freak her the fuck out. I know how inappropriate it is, especially in this situation, but my dick has a mind of its own when I'm around her.

If I'm being honest with myself, I've always had a thing for Quinn. It started after watching her for six months after the attack. No, that's not true. It really started before that when Walker pointed her out to me for the first time.

After that night, she'd been living in solitude under the radar and very pregnant. As I watched her body blossom, I was overtaken with such a need to protect her that rarely did I let anyone else guard her besides my boys or me.

The day that truly got to me was when she went to visit her parent's grave with flowers. As far away as I was, the devastation on her face was heartbreaking.

She spent a good half hour there and I watched as she touched her pregnant stomach under her winter coat. I knew that

she was telling them about the babies.
Yeah, I knew she was having twins. Even
with how they came to be, she still wanted
to keep them. I never figured out how she
became pregnant, as I was sure the hospital
would have taken precautions against it.
Obviously someone fucked up at the
hospital. Anyway, that strength showed me
how much good was in Quinn's heart. At
that moment, she owned mine.

Now as I stand at her bedside as she
slowly pulls herself together from yet
another nightmare, I can't hold back any
longer. I know it when she sees my
intentions as I pull the sheet back and climb
in bed next to her. She immediately tenses
up but doesn't move.

Keeping my eyes pinned to hers, I
very carefully reach for her, pulling her to
me – close, but not too close – so I don't
come on too strong and scare her away.
"It'll be ok. Trust me." I move her hair away
from her face and feel her body relaxing. As
I move my hands down to gently rub her
shoulders and back, she leans into me

slightly, letting out a sigh. Knowing that I'm on the right track, I keep rubbing up and down her back, slowly and innocently.

"Go to sleep, Quinn. I've got ya Sugar." She tucks in a bit closer to me, saying nothing. Within minutes, she's sleeping again. Knowing this is going to be a torturous night for me, I reach between us and adjust my length so it doesn't rub against her stomach. Just my hand moving my cock has it throbbing. *'Fuck,'* I think to myself, *'Cut me some slack.'*

I reach behind me to turn off the light, and at the same moment, she shifts her knee, brushing it across my cock. I can't stop the moan that escapes me as she wiggles closer. Trying to keep my groin away from her, I push back on the bed while she moves closer. Feeling that I'm fighting a losing battle, I decide I have no choice but to lay still. I put my hand to my mouth, fighting the urge to turn her over and fuck her hard, but that's the last thing she needs.

I've followed her for years. I know that she's had a few sexual encounters throughout the years, but none of them ever seemed to go beyond sex. It killed me, yet there was nothing I could do about it. She needed those encounters as part of the healing process. But now, being this close to her and not being able to touch her, regardless of the past, is fucking killing me.

I shift her hand away from my thigh and move to get out of bed, then I hear a soft giggle. I look and see Quinn watching me with a twinkle in her eye. She's playing with me. Leaning down, I whisper, "Girl, do you know what you're doing, 'cause this is no laughing matter. You're playing with fire so let me up and get some sleep."

"Sorry. I didn't mean to get you all hot and bothered. I didn't want to revisit my nightmare so I thought a bit of clowning around would take my mind off of it. Actually, I didn't expect you to react like this so I'm sorry. I'll be good, just please don't go. I'll go to sleep."

Considering what she says and how she goes from being silly to upset, I lay back down and turn my back to her. She does the same so we're back to back. I pray we can stay this way for the rest of the night.

CHAPTER 9

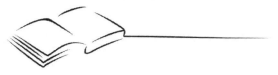

Feeling wrapped up in a warmth I've never felt before, I don't want to open my eyes and start another fucked up day, but I can't stay in this cocoon forever. Once my sleepy mind clears, I'm aware of the heat coming from the body that's wrapped around me like a snug jacket. His breath is softly tickling my neck and ear he's so close.

I'm surprised that I don't feel the usual panic, but my pulse is racing. Trying not to disturb Stone, I move to get out of bed and away from his tempting body. All those hard muscles, along with his morning wood is affecting me more than I want it to. Finally able to shift so my body can move from under his, I try to lift up and feel his fingers tighten on my hip, pulling me back to where I was moments ago. I can feel him pressing his cock into the crevice of my ass. Feeling the sudden heat in my core and a wetness between my legs, I pull myself from him and sit on the edge of the bed.

Stone immediately moves behind me hugging my back to his chest. "Morning, sugar. What's the matter?" A shudder runs through my body at his soft, sleep filled voice. It makes my body want more which pisses me off. I've never let any man affect me the way Stone is. My body is so in tune to his that my nipples are hard and my skin is scorching where his hands lay on my stomach, rubbing gently. Damn, he knows what to do. Feeling fucked, I shake my head, not wanting my voice to betray how much he's driving me insane.

"Did ya have another nightmare? You need to let me in so I can help you. That's all I want to do." Finally, not able to take anymore, I pull away and stand up so I can turn and face him and my mouth drops open.

He's sitting on the bed with no shirt, and apparently no boxers, either. All I can do is stare at his ripped muscles all along his body. I lick my bottom lip while looking at the V that draws my eyes to that spot between his legs. My eyes bulge as I see the slit of his cock glistening with drops of pre-cum. He's also long and thick with metal balls down the length of him which makes my core clench tightly, imaging the feeling of having him deep inside of me. Raising my eyes to his, I see he's amused. "Do you like what you see?"

Pissing me off with his arrogance, I reply with, "Not bad for a guy your age. Good to see that you're still able to function without the little blue pill." Giggling nervously because as usual, my mouth takes off before I can think. This seems to make him furious.

"What the fuck do you mean? Oh, that's right. You only fuck the young, stupid ones. The last guy was what, twenty-three? You like picking them up in bars, nice and drunk, don't ya."

Feeling like he kicked me in the stomach, I turn and run to the bathroom, slamming the door and locking it. I'm trembling and can't fathom how he knows who I've been with. Why I'm surprised, I don't know. He seems to have knowledge about every aspect of my life. Sitting on the toilet, holding my head in my hands, I take a time-out from him and this fucked up start to a new day. I need to clear my head and figure out what the plan for the day is.

Watching Quinn run away from me, I realize what an asshole comment that was. I didn't need to throw shit up in her face because I was pissed off and jealous. Damn. Sitting on the edge of the bed, it finally hits me what all the guys have been saying for years. Quinn's been in my sight for years and I've wanted her just as long. Something about her drew me to her. Not only is she gorgeous, but she has a heart of gold. She's protected her family all these years at the expense of her own happiness. The last couple of months has been pretty lonely for her. Seeing her eyes widen as she looked long and hard at my pierced cock was the reaction I was hoping for. She was excited.

I need to stop thinking with my dick and start getting my shit together 'cause we have a lot to do today, unfortunately. So, as for me getting some sort of release this morning, it's not gonna happen. Taking a deep breath, I concentrate on controlling my body.

Getting up, I make the bed and walk to the bathroom door, knocking softly. "Quinn, you ok in there? Look, I'm sorry. I didn't mean to step over that line and be a total asshole. It won't happen again, I promise." Hearing nothing, I knock again, "I'm gonna start some coffee so come out whenever you're ready." I leave her alone to gather herself, going into the kitchen to start the day.

CHAPTER 10

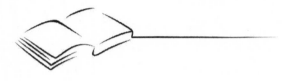

I enter the kitchen fully dressed, ready to face the day and more importantly, Stone. I find him making breakfast, but not just any breakfast. He's making all my favorites, including link turkey sausages with pancakes. Yeah, I guess he does know everything about me, and that sends a shiver down my spine as I quickly go through some of the things I wish he didn't know. Oh well, guess I'm shit out of luck at this point. You can't change the past no matter how much you want to. I know this as fact.

"Didn't know you could cook, Stone. You're going to make some girl a great wife someday." I smirk.

Not taking offense, he nods to the table, "Sit your fine ass down after you grab some coffee. I'll dish this up so we can work out our plans for today." After getting coffee and a plate full of food, I watch him sit across from me, stuffing pancakes into his mouth while watching me too. I put a piece of pancake in my mouth and moan. God, these are so good. Who knew, and since I'm starving, I dig in as we eat in silence until both plates are empty.

Stone grabs our empty plates and cleans up. He refills his coffee cup and asks, "You need a warm up?" Nodding, he fills mine too.

"I owe you an apology for earlier. Your choices are yours and I have no right to make comments, or worse, be disrespectful to your choices. It won't happen again." He waits for something, but I just nod my head, saying nothing, so he continues, "Today we'll get you packed, go to the bakery, and speak to Ivy. Then we'll get you to your sisters and the twins. Once there, we'll be moving all of you again to a safe house we have out in the country. Any questions so far?" Thinking about what he's just said, I ask the obvious, "Will I be able to contact Ivy during this time? And what happens if we don't want to go to your safe house. Are you going to force us?"

Understanding her concern and hesitation, I try to explain why it has to be this way. "Sugar, for your safety and all involved, it has to be this way. So to answer your questions, yes, you can contact Ivy on a burner phone." Seeing her confusion I continue, "A burner phone is one that can't be traced. For the safe house, we need you somewhere we have control of and have security measures in place." She agrees, but this is a small victory. This next one is gonna to be a battle. "Good. Now, let's handle the huge elephant in the room, and please hear me out before you say anything. I know probably everything there is to know about you. I know your daily routine, your business, and who you've dated." I take a deep breath continuing on awkwardly, "without being disrespectful Quinn let's just say I have knowledge of everything you've done personally since I've been on watch." Her head jerks up looking at me intently as she blushes when she realizes what I am telling her.

"I made a promise to your parent's memories and to myself after watching the horror you went through and my part in it that until this was over, I would protect you. Over the years you weren't even aware of how close your uncle and cousin got to all of you. That was because of our protection, but that's over and we have to plan accordingly, so I'm gonna jump right in and ask you. How bad do you want revenge? I've read the journals and know your plan to bring them down, but honestly, it'll never work in the real world. Yeah, it looks good written on paper, but to think you can get that close to those men from your past and be able to pull that off by yourself. Never gonna happen, 'cause once you get face to face with them, all of it'll come rushing back at ya. You'll be dead by the time you approach the first asshole. So, I'm gonna offer you some help so we can finally put this shit behind both of us. What do you think? Are you open to my suggestions? I think if we work together, I can promise you that once this is all over, you, your sisters, and the twins will be able to live your lives any way you want to without looking over your shoulder for the rest of your lives. The thing you need to understand though is that I run the operations and have your best interest at heart in everything I do. You might not believe it but I care for you—always have. I don't see that stopping anytime in the future, now that I've finally gotten to actually meet you."

Watching her eyes widen in shock, I finish, "With the help of my boys, we'll rid the earth of these assholes once and for all, but we can't leave any trace that it was us. We all have too much to lose. We, the boys and I, work for a special unit with the

government as I told you before so we have
to be careful. Don't get me wrong, we've
taken assholes out over the years, but those
were orders we had to follow. Never have
we gone off the radar to take criminals out
without an order. Being government
employees, I don't want any of us to lose
what we've worked so damn hard for over
the years." Taking in a breath, I watch the
emotions roll across her face.

　　"You care about me?" Is the first
thing out of her mouth? Out of all the shit I
laid on the table, the only thing she caught
was that I care for her. Fuck, if she only
knew. Knowing this isn't the right time, I
take a moment to try and explain to Quinn
my feelings without giving too much away.
"Yes, I care about you. After watching you
survive that night, it showed me how strong
you are. All you've got to do is look in the
mirror to see your outer beauty, but over the
years, I've also seen your inner strength.
That's your greatest gift, Sweetie. I've
watched ya with those kids of yours and
goddamn, you still love those babies

unconditionally, even knowing that one of the assholes who brutalized you is the father. I've been with women, even some short relationships, but to tell you the truth, none have ever measured up to my fantasies of you, Quinn. This was before I ever even saw this bratty attitude of yours." I end with a laugh.

I wait a few moment for her to digest what I've said. "I was just puttin' my cards on the table, so to speak. You're a sexy, intelligent, warm hearted woman and I don't know a man around who wouldn't see that and not want you. Now as for the rest, don't worry. We'll get this shit handled and make sure you and your family are safe."

"I'm actually at a loss for words, Stone, and that's something that never happens. You can ask anyone who knows me." She giggles, "I need some time to process what you've given me, but as to wanting revenge? Yes, I want it so we can all finally move forward with our lives, so whatever we can do to make that happen,

I'm ready for it. Do you have a plan?" she asks.

"We start today. We'll need to make sure that Raven has no contact with Walker 'cause this safe house is our only place that I know that he won't find. We need to figure out how tight your cousin's hold is on her. I have a real bad feeling knowing Walker. He may have abused or used her and is threating her in some way to keep a line of communication open. After we work all this out, we then figure out the best way to make those who hurt you pay. I can tell you that out of the nine men, besides Walker, only four are left."

"What do you mean, only four are left? Is that total five, including Walker? What happened to the others, Stone?"

Standing up, I tell her not to move as I go to into her family room and grab my computer bag. Coming back into the kitchen, I smirk to myself, seeing she actually did listen to me. Placing the bag on the table, I open it and pull out two laptops. Opening the gunmetal laptop, I turn it on and scroll for the information I can share with her. Finding it, I click on the file and refresh my memory on the facts. Once I have what I need, I turn my attention to Quinn. "There are four remaining, besides Walker, which makes five—all living free and breathing. One of the men was killed in an attempted robbery a year after your rape. Two of the others, who were brothers, were killed about 4 years ago during a drug raid. The other two have just disappeared, but from what we gathered from Walker's conversations, he had them taken out. Not sure why, but they're believed to be dead. Your cousin has kept the ones he knows will protect him, no matter what the cost, close. My plan is to either have the remaining ones arrested so they can spend the rest of their lives in jail, removing them from their wealth and resources. If we have no other choice, we just end their miserable lives. You need to think hard on how far you want to go with this because once we start, there's no going back."

Pulling my chair next to hers, I turn the laptop toward us and as soon as Quinn looks at the screen, seeing the pictures of the four remaining men who violated her, her face turns white as she pushes her chair back, jumps up and runs across the room with her hands to her face. FUCK! Didn't see that coming. I go to her and pull her to me, trying to console her the best I can as she quietly sobs. "Sugar, I'm so sorry. I didn't think for one moment seeing those assholes would be so hard on you. Come on, look at me." She raises her head from my chest; her tear filled eyes look up to me with so much agony. I gently wipe the tears off her cheeks, just as she leans her face into my hands so I'm holding her face. She continues to stare at me and suddenly the room fills with not only her panicked breaths, but also with the sexual tension between us. I don't know what to do. She's freakin' out over the damn pictures and I don't want her having a breakdown so I go to kiss her. I have no idea where it'll go from here, but I'm willing to see.

CHAPTER 11

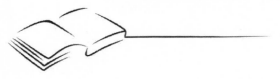

As I gaze into Stone's eyes, I can see the desire for me there. I've never been so affected by a man's stare. It feels like he's looking into my soul. He's shared everything with me. He's protected me over the years and may have real feelings for me, or what he thinks is the real me, makes me want more from him. I want to just let go for once in my life, but I know the timing is wrong. We have too much to do and I owe him an explanation as to why I am the way I am.

Taking a breath, I manage to get control over my raging desire for the man in front of me. Realizing what I'm about to do makes my body tremble. Feeling my

reaction, Stone naturally pulls me closer.
'Damn, this sucks,' I think to myself.
Finally, I have the desire for a man like a
normal woman and the timing is off.

Gently pushing on his muscular chest,
I grab his hands as he goes to drop them.
Giving them a soft squeeze, I move back to
my chair looking his way. "Sit for a bit,
Stone. I want to share some things with
you." Watching him move to the opposite
chair, I realize at that moment the control
and strength Stone has over his body. I can
see him struggling as he adjusts himself in
his jeans, looking for some relief. Trying to
clear my mind, I grab my coffee and take a
sip.

"I did put a lot of blame on you
because in my eyes, you did nothing but
watch. Fuck, Stone. They tortured me and
all you did was watch. After a while,
looking back and realizing you were one
person against how many, nine or ten? You
were right in assuming that if you busted in,
whether you were close to Walker or not, he
would have killed or tortured you for not

wanting to be a part of his demented revenge on my family. I never understood why you didn't call for help but now that you explained it to me, I'm kind of freaked out that after all this time, you and your *"friends"* have been watching my family. It's also scary to me that you've been so close and know so much about me. As you know, I'm a very private person and to know you have been in my home, watched personal things that I've done, and even read my journals, pisses me off and embarrasses me."

"Quinn, never be embarrassed. I never took anything I read in the journals and looked at you differently. You needed an outlet to release what had happened to you and to be able to function in society. I get that. Some of it was a bit disturbing in the beginning when you talked about how you would torture each one of those bastards, but I knew that was the grief and heartache talking, not you. As the years went on, your entries became less about revenge and more of a way to get your thoughts and feelings out in a healthy way. When you finally broke it down to the three journals, I knew that you were working to get past the nightmare. I came to the realization that you were moving on the first time you brought that guy home with you. I knew how big of a step this was for you, even though it tore me to pieces. That was one of the longest nights of my life. Just the thought of some fucker touching you – fucking you – made me nuts, but you were trying to live again so I stuck to just watching you and not interfering in your healing process."

All I can do is try and understand his side of things, so I squeeze his hands, letting him know I get it, and I appreciate all of it.

Watching Stone struggle with his story, it hits me that this man who has never met me personally, has been my Guardian Angel for years. He's seen me grow up, spread my wings, so to speak, and let my hair down a time or two. "Hey, that guy was a dud and he never made it to the bedroom that night. We made out on the couch and he prematurely jumped the gun, if you know what I mean. Guess I was too much for him." She softly laughs. "I got pissed off and showed him the door. That was my first attempt at having sex since Walker's shit and believe me, I went right back to my BOB's after that." I finish on a shy giggle.

"Why would you call them BOB's?" Laughing at the look on his face, I can't even begin to explain. The more I laugh, the worse he looks, so trying to get some control over myself, I move from the table to grab the coffee pot, filling both of our cups up. When I walk back to the table, I finally have some control.

"For a smart guy, you sure are a dumbass. BOB stands for Battery Operated Boyfriend, but since I have more than one BOB, I call them BOB's." He's got a huge shit-eating grin on his face and starts to laugh loudly breaking the tension between us because when he smiles, his face morphs into something beautiful.

Shaking my head to clear my mind of this sexy talk, I focus and start again. "I know your intentions have been honorable, but it doesn't change how I feel about you knowing my most personal thoughts. You know more than either of my sisters or Ivy even knows."

As I'm talking, a sudden thought pops into my head. Holy shit, I referenced the guy with green eyes in my journals through the years. Trying to remember what I said, I feel my face blushing because some of it was really personal, depending on if I was drunk or sober. So now he knows my thoughts about my fantasy green eyed guy from the entries I made in my journal. Now it makes sense how he could be so honest about how he felt. Stone has a head start to my thoughts and feelings from reading my journals.

"You know some of my feelings about you or specifically "my green-eyed guy" because of the journals, right? That's why you're comfortable enough to share what you're feeling because there's no pressure. I'm an open book, no pun intended. Just so you know, I've spoken to numerous counselors about those *"feelings"* and have been told that was one way that I handled the whole nightmare. It horrified me to think about you in anyway other than part of the worse night of my life. One counselor explained it to me as a form of Asperger's Syndrome. Not being involved in the actual torture my mind came to associate you as my only support that helped me during that horrible traumatic event in my life. It took years to realize that you really didn't support me at all, actually you did nothing or that is what I assumed until you explained it to me yesterday."

Grabbing my mug, I immediately stand up and go to the sink to rinse it out. "I really need some time to think about everything you've said and I don't want you here to do it. Give me some *me* time to let this penetrate. Can you do that for me?"

Not waiting for his answer, I walk directly to my bedroom, pushing the door closed behind me. I don't bother with waiting to hear for the click indicating it locked. Going around the bed to the nightstand with my most recent journals, I lay down and hold the three books close to my heart. This is how I've survived all these years. I have boxes of journals in my basement. One therapist had said that writing stuff down took away the power of the memory tied to it. It worked for me, so why stop when something was working? I grab and open the blue journal and with my hands shaking, I grab a pen and write one word in capital letters, *STONE.*

CHAPTER 12

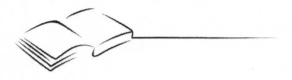

After taking some time to reflect, I realize that I'm not really mad at Stone, just more embarrassed than anything. I'm mad at myself for some of things I have written in the journals over the years—Steamy shit that he had no right to read about as I didn't like being so exposed. Putting down on paper my fantasies is one thing, since I have an overactive imagination when it comes to shit like that, but never did any of my fantasies come close to this man driving me so fucking crazy. Damn, my mouth waters just envisioning him naked on my bed again. I can only image how his piercing green eyes would look down on me as he took me.

Now is not the time to think about the sexual tension between Stone and me. Unfortunately my body isn't on the same page as my sexual need as it had me in knots and needed to be released quickly as there was so much I needed to do and at the moment couldn't think straight let alone function. So with him gone, I figure this is as good a time as any to relieve this pressure so my brain can function. Even with everything going on, I need this, just something to take the edge off quickly before he comes back.

Reaching into my nightstand, I pull out one of my BOB's. Running him down my tummy to the spot that needs him the most, I turn him on and get to work. Goddamn, I need a release and fast.

Closing my eyes, I feel Bob hitting the right spot as I put some pressure on the tip of my vibrator so it presses into my clit. I let out a small moan as I begin to chase my orgasm. My core clenches as my body tells me I'm close. Feeling myself getting wetter by the minute, I start to pump BOB in and out of my clenching vagina then put him back on my throbbing clit as I feel the beginning of my orgasm.

"What the fuck are you doin'? Holy shit, that's so fuckin' hot—don't stop, keep going."

I scream at the sound of his voice, which shocks the hell out of me as BOB goes flying landing between my pillows at the head of the bed. Unfortunately, I didn't get a chance to turn him off so now my pillows are humming with a steady buzz. Embarrassed as hell, I scrunch my forehead tight and grind my teeth together, putting my hands over my eyes as I pray he just leaves. Shit, I thought the door locked behind me.

I wait for him to leave but when I don't hear anything, I peek through my fingers and can't fucking believe my eyes. Holy shit this can't be happening. What the fuck, he is masturbating, leaning against the door jamb, pants undone and has his length in his hand as he goes up and down while looking at me. I'm mesmerized and can't look away. His hand runs over the tip covered in pre-cum and uses it to moisten his cock. His hand glides up and down smoothly and then he stops mid-glide to play with his piercings.

We stare at each other until his lips move and a small smirk appears. "We've got a lot of shit to do today and as much as my body's telling me to join you on that bed and fuck you into tomorrow, it ain't gonna happen. If and when it does, I plan for it to be a slow, sensual process, not a wham-bam thank you fuck. So do me a favor and finish yourself off while I watch you so we can take care of what we need to. Don't even think of asking me to leave 'cause it ain't happenin'. It's taking everything in me to stay here so I'm begging you, continue what you were doing and let me watch you like I have dreamt about for fuckin' years Quinn."

Feeling every word he says as if he's touching me, I continue to stare into those green eyes that always seem to be watching me always. Struggling because of my mixed feelings for Stone I can't fight my own needs and desires even not knowing how I will feel afterward. Reaching for BOB I turn him off shocked that I would even consider this form of voyeurism, I move my hand down past my stomach as his eyes follow. Knowing that I'll do as he's asked, my fingers find my clit and start to rub up and down, then round and round until my hips are pumping into my hand.

Stone continues to work his length but his eyes remain on me. Having him watch me brings my orgasm that much quicker and before I know it, I'm clenching around my fingers and screaming out my release. Trying to keep my eyes on Stone, I watch as his hand works up and down, faster and faster until finally he reaches his own release. He has the most beautiful expression etched across his face in that moment.

Stone's not at all embarrassed that I watched him beat off as I realization of what just happened hits me. He takes a minute to bring his breathing back to normal and grins. "Now that is the right way to wake up in the morning or get over a fight. Just fuck it out."

Feeling a bit of relief I laugh at his comment because he's too cute for his own sake. The uncomfortable sexual tension between us is gone, even though we have so many more issues to overcome but for now I think we can finally move on with our day.

CHAPTER 13

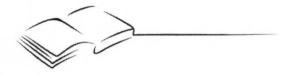

After our crazy masturbation session, we reconvene in the kitchen to plan the day out. Stone decides I should call Ivy first to make sure all is well at my bakery before we head there, so I follow orders and Ivy picks up immediately. "Are you ok, Quinn? How was your night? Did you get some sleep? Are you coming in today?"

"Ivy, take a fucking breath. We'll be there in about an hour or so. Have one of the other's start the days baking as we are going to need to change up some schedules. I'll explain as I have to bring you up to speed with what's going on, ok?"

I hear her talking to someone in the background before she answers. "Yeah, that's cool. What do you mean we'll? Whose we'll? I'm here so take your time. I'm not going anywhere. My partner works me like a dog." I hear the laughter in her tone. "We never get a fucking day off, but that's ok. Damn, my partner truly isn't that bad, but don't tell her I said so." Giggling at how stupid she is sometimes, I ask if there were any problems or issues with any strange people. As it always is between us, we start talking about this that until I feel Stone at my back, obviously waiting for me. I say my goodbye to Ivy, informing her I'll be by shortly.

Stone grabs my hand and pulls me to the couch. "Let's get this started, sound like a plan?" He asks.

I shake my head, knowing we're about to embark on a journey where no one knows how it's going to end. Knowing that Stone and his guys have had our backs and will continue in the future, gives me some feelings of peace and security that I haven't had since that night. So yes, I'm grabbing onto this with both hands and not letting go. Finally knowing that I'm going to be able to get my revenge on the assholes that ruined my life and took my parents from us is a good feeling. Knowing that Walker is going to go down for his part in their deaths and my violation is even better. After all these years of existing but not truly living is over.

With Stone's help, maybe I can finally move forward and get away from my past and be more in the present. With the help of my journals and Stone, this phase in my life will finally be coming to end.

COMING SOON

Quinn's story continues
In the Present titled Vengeance
Book Two of The Journals Trilogy.

Thank you for your purchase of Anguish. I hope you have enjoyed it and if so, please leave a review on the purchasing site in which you've purchased it. Reviews do not need to be long – a couple of sentences – stating your thoughts on this book. Each review helps me as an author attract new readers.

ABOUT THE AUTHOR

D. M. Earl resides in Northwest Indiana. An avid reader since childhood she has taken the next steps to start writing professionally. When not reading or writing D.M. can be found on her 04 Harley hitting the road beside her husband riding his own 2011 Harley. She also enjoys being outdoors gardening or working in one of her many flowerbeds. An avid pet lover D.M. can be found on her back deck with her two pits laying at her feet enjoying the sun and chimes as the indoor cats look out. There are also multiple strays living in their garage and her & her husband feed the wildlife in the area.

If you would like to contact me, please do so at dmearl14@gmail.com, or by snail mail:

> D. M. Earl
> P.O. Box 306
> Dyer, Indiana 46311

Below are my social media links to stay in contact and hear about all my works in progress and upcoming releases. You can find me on Facebook, Amazon, Twitter, TSU, and Goodreads.

Facebook (Like) http://bit.ly/dmearl14

Amazon http://bit.ly/amazondmearl

Twitter http://bit.ly/twitterdmearl

TSU http://bit.ly/tsudmearl

Goodreads http://bit.ly/goodreadsdmearl

I'm also including my newsletter and website in case you would like to sign up for updates on a monthly basis.

Newsletter-http://bit.ly/newsletterdmearl

Website https://dmearl.com

WHEELS & HOGS SERIES

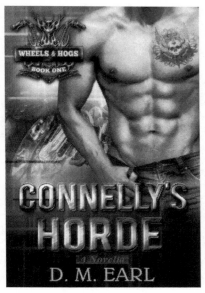

Welcome to Desmond Connelly's Horde or better known as his extended family at Wheels & Hogs Garage. For years these survivors have been dealing with what life throws them while trying to move forward from the atrocities in their lives. Some have secrets not shared while others are working through problems that are continually present in their lives.

Follow Des as he introduces you to each one of his crew at Wheels & Hogs in this short Novella. Start to understand how a group of strangers become not only friends but family over the years. Get a snapshot of why when life pushes you down, in this garage, you push back until you are on your feet again.

Connelly's Horde
http://amzn.to/1DNnMD5

Cadence Powers is tattooed, pierced, and panty dropping gorgeous. Women love him and men want to be him. It appears to the world that he has it all, but what people don't see is that Cadence is a damaged haunted man, held back by untold secrets that keep him from living a real life.

When he meets Trinity Vinkers, he feels as if he can finally live the life he desperately wants. However, just as their friendship begins to grow, one stupid act causes that friendship to shatter, all because he lets his guard down allowing her into his life.

Trinity appears to be the light to Cadence's dark. Innocent, naïve, and goofy, she seems to bring out the best in everyone around her, but she has her own dark secret. Her persona allows her to fake her way through life, at least until she meets him. Trying not to let her feelings for Cadence get the best of her is taken out of her hands when she makes a wrong decision that leaves her left with an unexpected fallout.

As life takes both Cadence and Trinity down a path that neither will forget, they are unaware of the evil lurking around them. It's watching, waiting to step in and take everything from Cadence.

As the young lovers struggle with their secrets, a close friend will also be fighting for something,... her life. As time goes by, Cadence and the Horde from Wheels & Hogs decide that they have to do whatever it takes to keep what is theirs safe, even as death hovers around like a dark angel.

Cadence Reflection
http://amzn.to/1IHQW7D

Gabriel "Doc" Murphy found the woman he'd planned to treasure for the rest of his life in a young, shy girl he had seen being bullied in a hallway between classes when they were just kids. Over the years, Doc loved and protected her with all he had, until the day came when he received news that there was something that could take her away from him...Cancer. Being faced with the possibility of losing the love of his life, Doc would turn the world inside-out to save and keep the only love that could shatter him, body and soul, if he couldn't save her.

Fern knew the instant she fell into Gabriel's arms all those years ago, that she had found her "one and only." He became her everything-owning her heart and soul. As they made it through their life journey together, nothing could tear their unbreakable bond. Life struggles, financial losses, and even devastating miscarriages didn't stand a chance until the day she received the phone call that finally shattered their world to the core, leaving Fern preparing for the fight of her life.

As Doc and Fern struggle through each day, praying for a miracle, one presents itself. Do they dare have hope, or do they accept that the fight is over as a dark shadow waits patiently to make a move to alter their lives forever.

COMING SOON

Gabriel's Treasure
add to GOODREADS

http://bit.ly/1G71KJN

Made in the USA
Lexington, KY
02 April 2017